Glamour Girl

Aquaria Newton

Table of Contents

Chapter 1
The Sparkle Begins

The first time Tia Morgan felt her life could be genuinely extraordinary was the afternoon she and her best friend, Kayla, walked through the bustling Paradise Mall. It was a Saturday, one of those days where the world felt a little brighter; the possibilities seemed endless.

"I'm telling you, Tia," Kayla said, holding one hand up to balance a tray of pretzels while waving the other hand around like a maniac, "you could totally do the cover of Teen Glow. You've got the height, the hair and that whole mysterious vibe. Like, hello? Instant model!"

Tia shook her head and laughed. "No, Kayla, I'm awkward, so I'm mysterious. Models are, you know… poised. Glamorous. Not me."

Kayla rolled her eyes. "You're beautiful, and you don't even know it. You have, trust me, the right look. All you need is—"

"Excuse me," someone broke in.

Tia, surprised, turned to face a lean woman wearing sharp red frames and sophisticated black clothes standing directly in front of them. She carried a clipboard and strode with some serious boss energy.

"Are you two locals?" the woman said, eyes roaming over Tia with interest.

"Y-yeah," Tia stammered.

"Good! Classic," the woman said, smiling confidently. "I am Simone DeVoe, a talent scout for Star Style Agency. Next week, we are holding auditions for an upcoming Teen Fashion Show, and I think you…," she pointed right at Tia. "Would be perfect."

Kayla gasped, so loudly that people at the pretzel stand looked over at her. "Oh. My. Gosh. Did you hear that, Tia? PERFECT!"

1

Tia blinked, her face hot. "Wait… me? Are you sure?"

Simone chuckled. "I have spent the last decade scouting talent, and I know when I see potential. Here." She passed Tia a glossy flyer. "The audition is on Wednesday after school. Be there by 4 p.m. sharp. Bring this flyer and wear something basic but fashionable. We'll take it from there."

After a final nod, Simone left, and Tia stood frozen.

Kayla had gripped her shoulders and shaken her. "Tia! Do you know what just happened? You got scouted. Like, for real! This is your big moment!"

"I don't know," Tia said uncertainly, looking at the leaflet. It was printed in big, glittery letters: Teen Fashion Show Auditions: Shine Like the Star You Are!

"What do you mean you don't know?!" Kayla exclaimed. "This is huge! You've gotta do it!"

Tia sighed. "It's just… I don't think I'm a 'shine like a star' type of person. I trip on my own feet, Kayla. And what if I mess up? Or worse, what if they mock me?"

Kayla folded her arms. "First of all, you're not tripping. You're stepping into your destiny. And secondly, if anyone laughs at you, I'm going to deal with them myself." She dramatically flexed her arms, a gesture that made Tia laugh through her nerves.

"I don't know," Tia said softly again, putting the flyer into her bag.

Tia wondered if Kayla was right as the two friends left the mall. Was this her opportunity to be the quiet, invisible girl everyone ignored?

Tia lay in bed that night staring at the ceiling, the words Simone had used ringing in her head. "You would be perfect!"

Maybe, she thought as she dropped off to sleep, just maybe, this was her moment to show she could be glittery after all.

4

Chapter 2
The Glam Squad

By Wednesday afternoon, Tia's stomach was like a gymnastics tournament. One hand clutched the flyer while the other tugged at the hem of her favorite jean jacket. Kayla had helped her choose a simple but cute outfit: skinny jeans, a white tank top and her trusty sneakers. "You look so effortlessly cool," Kayla had said. But Tia didn't feel cool. She wanted to run home.

Star Style Agency's building was sleek and modern, its glass windows stretching from floor to ceiling, brightened even more by the sunlight outside. Inside, the lobby buzzed with activity. Girls of every shape in various outfit styles filled the room. Some were chattering excitedly, and others were practicing their walks in sky-high heels.

"Okay, Tia," she mumbled to herself, "just breathe. You've got this."

The sound of a clipboard closing made her jump. A hard-looking woman with a bun and no-nonsense face stood to in the front of the room." "Ladies, listen up! I am your audition coordinator, Miss Janelle. We want confidence, poise and personality. If you survive today, you can join the Teen Fashion Show cast. Good luck!"

When the auditions started, the girls were divided into clusters of five. Tia's group consisted of a bubbly redhead named Mia, a quiet girl named Leila and two other girls — one of whom was Chanel. Channeling the era with perfectly coiffed hair and full glam makeup, she appeared as though plucked from the pages of an old-school fashion mag.

"Hi, I'm Tia," she blurted nervously, wanting to seem friendly.

Chanel barely glanced at her. "Chanel," she muttered, flipping her long hair.

Mia folded in closer to Tia and whispered, "Don't listen to her. She thinks she's Beyoncé."

Tia stifled a laugh. She liked Mia already.

When it was time for Tia to walk the runway, her heart pounded in her chest. She kept her mind on Miss Janelle's directions: "Shoulders back, chin up, walk with purpose."

Mia took the stage first, her grin illuminating the room. Then Chanel arrived, looking like she owned the place. Leila stumbled slightly but was quickly back on her feet. And then it was Tia's turn.

She swallowed hard, stepped onto the runway and, as bravely as she could, walked. In the beginning, the effort felt a little awkward, but then she recalled Kayla's words: "You're walking into your destiny." By the time she finished her walk, she had even cracked a little smile.

6

You're walking into your destiny !!!

7

Once everyone was done, Miss Janelle began to announce the names of the people who advanced to the next round. Tia's heart was pounding as she waited.

"Mia Carter, Chanel Dupree, Leila Martinez, and … Tia Morgan!"

Tia's knees almost gave out. She made it.

The girls who were chosen were taken to another room and handed folders with their rehearsal and fitting schedules. Chanel rolled her eyes at Mia, applauding everyone, but Tia just smiled. For the first time in her life, she belonged.

On the way out, Chanel looked at Tia. "Nice job… for a beginner. But don't settle in too comfortably. Not everybody is meant for this."

Tia opened her mouth to speak, but Mia interjected. "Ignore her, Tia. She's just frightened you will eclipse her."

Tia chuckled tentatively, but the reality was Chanel's remarks stung. Did she really have what it takes to hang with girls like Chanel?

As she reviewed the rehearsal schedule that night, Tia made a vow to herself: no matter what, she was going to give everything to the experience.

Chapter 3
Lights, Camera, Drama

Rehearsals started the following day, and Tia's high from successfully getting through the auditions turned quickly into stress overload. Mirror-lined walls, every movement made sharp and loud by the whip-like directions of Miss Janelle as she paced the floor like a drill sergeant.

"Posture, ladies! Shoulders back! You're not meandering through the mall, you're walking the runway!'

Tia struggled to keep up. From the first to the latter half of the song, This Is Everything, she kept missing the beat in the choreography, and her steps never quite matched those of the other girls. Chanel, meanwhile, glided around the room as though she were born in heels, casting a smug side-eye in Tia's direction every time she stuttered.

"Focus, Tia!" Miss Janelle barked. "You're hesitating. Trust your movements."

Tia nodded, her face burning. She had struggled to hide the nerves, and Chanel's whispered comment didn't make things any better. "Maybe modeling isn't for everyone," she muttered just loudly enough for Tia to hear.

By the rehearsal's end, Tia felt exhausted and disheartened. With that, she collapsed onto a bench next to Mia, who passed her a water bottle.

"Don't let Chanel get to you," Mia said. "She's just insecure. She's probably afraid you will outshine her."

"Oh, yeah?" said Tia, her eyes rolling. "I can't even walk in a straight line.

Mia grinned. "Neither could I before I did. It takes practice. Besides, you've got something Chanel does not."

"What's that?"

"A personality," Mia said with a wink.

Tia laughed despite herself. Maybe Mia was right.

The following week went by in a blur of rehearsals, fittings and photoshoots. Tia began to gain confidence until one afternoon in practice, a catastrophe occurred.

It was a five-step routine: walk, spin, throw your arms up. Tia had just nailed the spin when Chanel "accidentally" collided with her, knocking her to the floor.

"Oh no," Chanel said, feigning shock. "So sorry, Tia! I didn't see you there."

10

Laughter rippled in the room, and Tia's cheeks burned.

Miss Janelle gave a hand clap. "Focus, ladies! No time for distractions. Tia, stand back up and try again.

Fighting back tears, Tia stood up. Chanel's smirk felt like a burning ember on her back, but she wouldn't let it break her. She completed the routine, her steps shaky but determined.

After their rehearsal, Mia and Leila ran into her in the hallway.

"Chanel's so a diva," Leila said, frowning. "You dealt with that a lot better than I would have."

"Barely," Tia said, her voice shaking. "She is so mean — I don't get it."

"Because she's jealous," Mia said confidently. "When people need to put others down, they are usually insecure. Don't let her win, Tia."

Tia nodded, but the doubt remained. What if Chanel was right? What if she didn't even belong here?

The following day, Tia came early to practice. She was intent on NOT proving to herself or anybody else that she couldn't do this. For an hour, she walked the runway by herself, working on her posture, her steps, and her confidence.

By the time the others got there, she said, she was more ready. Even Chanel's barbed looks couldn't dislodge her.

"Tia," Miss Janelle added. "Much better today."

"Keep it up."

For the first time, a glimmer of frustration appeared in Chanel's eyes. And for the first time, Tia smiled to herself. Perhaps she did have what it took after all.

Chapter 4
True Colors

With each passing day, Tia tasted more and more success in her new job. Rehearsals stopped being scary, and she even started to have fun. Mia and Leila quickly became her closest companions, and the three of them would often remain after hours to hone their skills together.

But all of it was not smooth sailing. Chanel's attitude turned more and more petty. She rolled her eyes whenever Tia spoke, cracked snide remarks during breaks, and once "forgot" to pass along a critical schedule change, leading Tia to arrive late to a fitting.

Tia tried to ignore her and instead concentrated on her growing self-assurance. But one afternoon, two days before the fashion show, she overheard something that set her blood boiling.

"Make sure Mia's not there on time for the dress rehearsal," Chanel whispered to one of her friends, a girl named Veronica. "I'll handle the rest. There's no way she's taking my shine."

Tia froze. Chanel's plan made her stomach knot.

15

That night, she was in her room, replaying the scene. She knew she needed to do something, but confronting Chanel seemed scary. What if Chanel turned the other girls on her? What if Miss Janelle believed she was creating drama?

Her phone buzzed. It was a text from Kayla.

Kayla: "How's my future superstar? Ready to rock the runway?"

Tia sighed and texted back.

Tia: "Not really. Chanel's being Chanel again. Then she's going to mess with Mia."

Kayla replied a few seconds later.

Kayla: "Ugh. What's her deal? You HAVE to say something, Tia. You're better than her, and you know it."

Tia stared at the screen. Kayla was right. She couldn't let Chanel's jealousy ruin things for Mia — or anybody — so she sat with the child instead.

The following afternoon, Tia got to practice early and went directly to Miss Janelle.

"I must tell you something," Tia said, trembling. "It's about Chanel."

Miss Janelle gave the brow a raise. "Go on."

Tia paused to take a breath, then went through everything she'd heard. Miss Janelle absorbed this news silently behind an inscrutable expression.

"Thank you for bringing this to my attention, Tia," she said at last. "I'll handle it. And just so you know, it is brave to advocate for others. Well done."

Tia felt some relief, but she remained nervous. What if Chanel learned she had told?

At rehearsal, Miss Janelle huddled with the group before they started.

"Ladies, I just have to remind you that this is a team effort. Sabotage and other forms of undermining another participant will not be tolerated. I demand professionalism from everyone. Understood?"

Chanel's gaze flicked toward Tia, her face frostbitten. Tia's heartbeat quickened, but she stayed strong.

Chanel had been uncharacteristically quiet during practice. She steered clear of Tia and Mia, and her regular self-satisfaction was replaced by a strained smile.

Mia had no idea what had transpired but took Tia aside during a break. "You are walking with so much more confidence these days! Seriously, Tia, you're crushing it."

"Thanks," Tia said, smiling. "So are you."

By the time Tia finished rehearsal, she had learned a valuable lesson — it may not always be easy to stand up for what's right, but it was worth it. She wasn't merely discovering her confidence on the runway. She was discovering it in herself.

Chapter 5
The Path to Confidence

Destroying the mood of the day had been a very tall order for a walk down the runway. Behind the scenes, Stylists were bustling up and down furiously, rearranging outfits and patches in makeup. In the air hung the smells of hairspray, the sharp buzz excited conversation.

While Tia faced the mirror, she took the whole thing in. She wore a silver dress that shone brightly under the bright lights, with soft waves in her hair and makeup that was as subtle as it was radiant. At last, she felt that she truly belonged.

"You look fantastic," said Mia, appearing behind her in an audacious, emerald-green dress.

"So do you," laughed Tia. "Ready to rock this?"

Mia grinned. "Born ready."

As the music started, Tia peeped from behind a curtain. The audience was enormous - the biggest she had ever played to. She felt her heart thumping as the announcer announced the first group of models.

"Keep calm," she whispered. "You've got this."

Looking along the line of her as she stepped onto the runway, a bright glare momentarily blinded Tia's eyes. She concentrated hard on the rhythm of the music, letting her movements be guided by its tempo. Shoulders back and head held high, walk with determination-that's what Miss Janelle had taught her to do.

Halfway down the runway, she caught a glimpse of Kayla in the crowd, enthusiastically waving. Tia couldn't help but smile.

When she reached the far end of the runway, the initial nerves had gone. She struck a final pose and was immediately filled with an ecstasy of self-confidence she had never known. As she turned to walk back, the applause was thunderous and quite genuine.

Backstage, Mia was waiting for her, grinning. "You did great, Tia!"

"So did you!" Tia said, giving her a hug.

The last walk, when all the models returned to the runway together, was ecstatic; it just felt indescribable. As the music swelled, Tia felt proud and a sense of accomplishment. She had done it. When the show came to an end, the girls gathered backstage for the results.

Miss Janelle stepped forward, holding a microphone."Before I announce the winners," she said, "I want to congratulate all of you from the bottom of my heart. I can't tell you how much this industry needs fresh faces like yours."Every woman had her day. Chanel picked up the "Best Walk" award with a forced smile. Mia won "Most Charismatic," and who could be happier than Tia?

"One more thing," Miss Janelle said, "Finally, the award for 'New Star' goes to Tia Morgan!"

Tia stopped short, her eyes growing wider and wider. But Mia gave her a little nudge. "Go on, Tia!" She approached the podium to accept her award, heart thumping in her chest.

"Thank you," she said, her voice shaking with gratitude. "This experience has taught me so much about myself, not just as a model but also as a person who believes in herself. I am really very grateful for the chance to be here."The applause was deafening.

That night, when Tia sat together with Kayla, Mia and the rest of them to celebrate at an after-party, she felt...

"You know," she said, giving a smile, "It's precisely because I used to think that glamour was nothing more than being perfect in appearance or acting self-possessed that I think now it really means feeling self-confident and then spending the effort of helping everyone else around."Kayla lifted her Coke bottle in a toast.

"Here's to Tia Morgan, the true glamour girl!" Mia laughed and clinked her glass together with Kayla's. "And here's to kindness, courage and a dream that chases!"

She laughed and sang to the stars, arcing out for their photo (laughs). Trying various poses at home, Tia finally realized that he didn't have to compare herself with anyone else because, in fact, there is no comparison. She was herself, and enough, that was all. It was lovely, and that was the most glamorous of all.

The End

VOCABULARY

Vocabulary that aligns with the book's theme of beauty, confidence, friendships, and growth

Glamour (noun)	A quality of beauty, charm, or sophistication that is often enhanced by elegance, poise, and charisma. *Example: Her glamour was undeniable, and everyone admired her confidence*
Confidence (noun)	A feeling of self-assurance that comes from within, based on belief in one's abilities or qualities. *Example: With a strong sense of confidence, she walked into the room without hesitation.*
Elegance (noun)	The quality of being graceful, stylish, and sophisticated in appearance or manner. *Example: Her elegance in both speech and action made her the center of attention at every event.*
Self-acceptance (noun)	The recognition and acceptance of one's own worth, flaws, and uniqueness. *Example: Through her journey, she learned the importance of self-acceptance, realizing she was enough as she was.*
Resilience (noun)	The ability to recover or bounce back from difficulties, adversity, or challenges. *Example: Despite facing many setbacks, her resilience made her stronger than ever.*

Empowerment (noun)	The process of gaining confidence and control over one's life or circumstances. *Example: The book's message of empowerment encouraged the girls to believe in their dreams.*
Authenticity – (noun)	The quality of being genuine, true to oneself, and not pretending to be something else. *Example: She always valued authenticity, refusing to conform to others' expectations.*
Kindness (noun)	The quality of being friendly, generous, and considerate toward others. *Example: Acts of kindness spread throughout the group, making everyone feel valued and loved.*
Mentorship (noun)	The guidance and support given by an experienced individual to someone less experienced. *Example: Her mentor's advice helped her navigate the tough moments with grace and confidence.*
Perseverance (noun)	Steady persistence in a course of action, especially in spite of difficulties or delays in achieving success. *Example: The character's perseverance in reaching her goals inspired everyone around her.*
Self-love (noun)	The regard for one's own well-being and happiness, often including practices that enhance physical, mental, and emotional health. *Example: She realized that self-love wasn't selfish; it was necessary for her happiness and growth.*

Dignity (noun)	The quality of being worthy of honor and respect, often reflected in a person's conduct and demeanor. *Example: She handled the situation with dignity, never losing her composure in the face of criticism.*
Independence (noun)	The state of being free from reliance on others and being self-sufficient in one's decisions and actions. *Example: Her independence allowed her to make decisions that aligned with her values and goals.*
Supportive (adjective)	Providing encouragement, assistance, or backing to others in a way that helps them succeed. *Example: The group of friends was always supportive, celebrating each other's successes and offering help during tough times.*
Inspiration (noun)	The process of being mentally stimulated to do or feel something, especially something creative or positive. *Example: Her story became an inspiration for others, motivating them to chase their dreams.*
Legacy (noun)	Something handed down or passed on from one generation to another, often representing values, traditions, or accomplishments. *Example: The character strived to create a legacy of kindness, grace, and strength that others would remember.*

Charisma (noun)	A special magnetic charm or appeal that inspires others to follow or admire you. *Example: Her charisma was evident as soon as she entered the room, drawing people toward her with ease.*
Compassion (noun)	Sympathetic concern and a desire to help those who are suffering or in need. *Example: Her compassion for others shone through in the way she always listened and offered help.*
Self-doubt (noun)	A lack of confidence in one's own abilities or decisions. *Example: Overcoming self-doubt was one of the greatest challenges she faced in her journey to success.*
Inclusion (noun)	The practice of ensuring that all people, regardless of differences, are involved and valued. *Example: The group was a model of inclusion, making sure everyone had a voice and felt accepted.*

QUESTIONS

1. What qualities do you think make someone a "glamour girl"?

2. How does the book portray beauty beyond physical appearance?

3. In Glamour Girl, how do the characters define success and confidence? Do you agree with their definitions?

4. What does it mean to be glamorous, and how can someone embody this in everyday life?

5. Which character in the book do you relate to the most and why?

6. What role do friendship and support play in the journey of the glamour girls?

7. How do the characters overcome challenges in the book, and what can we learn from their experiences?

8. What are some ways we can celebrate individuality and uniqueness in our own lives?

9. What does the book teach about the importance of kindness, and how does it impact the characters?

10. How do you think the message of the book applies to young people today?

Author's Note

Dear Readers,

I wrote **"Glamour Girl"** for every girl who ever questioned her worth, her beauty, or her voice. As an educator, mentor, pageant director, kids' life coach and now author, I've seen firsthand how society often tells girls who they should be but rarely gives them space to discover who they are. Tia's journey as well as the other characters were inspired by real girls I've worked with, and the struggles many of us quietly carry behind our smiles and sparkles. This book is my way of saying: You are enough. You are seen. You are glamorous in every way that matters. Thank you for walking this journey with Tia and with me. I hope you see a piece of your story in hers and feel inspired to shine in your beautiful way.

With love, Aquaria

Reader's Affirmation

1. Shine From Within.
2. Speak these daily. Write them. Own them. Live them.
3. Affirm Like a Glamour Girl.
4. I am beautiful inside and out.
5. I am worthy of love, respect, and kindness.
6. I am allowed to grow, change, and dream big.
7. I don't have to be perfect to be powerful.
8. My story matters and so does my voice.
9. I shine from within and that shine is unstoppable.
10. I am beautiful just as I am.
11. I am enough. I believe in myself.
12. I have a voice, and it matters.
13. I am smart, strong, and unstoppable.
14. I choose kindness toward myself and others.
15. I celebrate my uniqueness.
16. I grow through every challenge.
17. I don't need to compare myself to anyone.
18. I am allowed to say no.
19. I am proud of who I'm becoming.
20. I treat myself with love and respect.

Reader's Affirmation Continuation

21. I attract good people and have good energy. I radiate confidence.
22. I rise above negativity.
23. I am bold enough to dream big.
24. I am worthy of good things.
25. I forgive myself and keep moving forward.
26. I walk with purpose and passion.
27. I am grounded, grateful, and growing.
28. I sparkle with grace and grit. I was born to shine. I am magic.
29. I am movement.
30. I am more.
31. I am a Glamour Girl, and I glow from within.

SHEVOLVES
ENTERPRISE

About the SHEvolves Movement

SHEvolves is more than a brand, it is a movement to empower girls and women to embrace their inner queen. Founded by Aquaria, SHEvolves hosts self-development camps, workshops, and events that build confidence, creativity, and community. From the classroom to the runway, every girl deserves to be seen, heard and celebrated.

Want to get involved?

Join a SHEvolves event

Book a workshop or school visit

Partner or sponsor a girl's journey

Let's evolve together because when she evolves, we all rise.

Follow us on Instagram: @shevolves_enterprise Email:

shevolvesenterprise@gmail.com

QR Code Invitation Page Scan & Connect with the Glamour Girl Community!

Be part of the movement!

Scan the QR code below to access your: Exclusive video message from Aquaria Updates on Behind the Glam Invites to upcoming SHEvolves events

Let's stay connected, inspired, and glamorously evolving together.

@SHEVOLVES_ENTERPRISE

31

Puzzle

Glamour Girl Vibes

Find these words:

CONFIDENCE, SHINE, BEAUTIFUL, BOLD, UNIQUE, EMPOWER, VOICE, QUEEN, KIND, GROWTH

```
G T C C O G K T R P G J
K G A O W L B Q T J E T
G W B N N U O U N X M P
R B A F N Q L E V V P B
O S V I D N D E A O O E
W H V D E X X N Z I W A
T I I E H X U W Y C E U
H N S N G J N Z W E R T
K E H C N V I V M K K I
O E E E F V Q Y X I S F
M I X E W L U A I N N U
N Z K E G O E Y M D F L
```

Friendship & Feelings

Find these words:

HONEST, LOYAL, TRUST, SUPPORT, LAUGH, TALK, LISTEN, APOLOGIZE, RESPECT, BOND

```
H A P O L O G I Z E H G
G P W I L I S T E N I U
Z U S N H O N E S T T B
G Z E C T L K N B L H O
Y B Q U R X H I Q R P N
L R X S U P P O R T G D
O S H R S N Q X G B E X
Y I J U T Z D E C L P J
A X J U E B G J B A T B
L R E S P E C T O U A K
E R H S C B A U U G L U
Q U R Z R G Q Q P H K G
```

Inner Power

Find these words:

STRONG, BRAVE, LEADER, SMART, DREAM, FOCUS, GOAL, HOPE, PEACE, WORTHY

```
T E Y W G A G U D V G C
E Y A O O B A V B M V I
M F Y R A R X I E M Z F
N Z F T L A U O Q F P Z
L O M H Y V W Y C I E Z
Q C V Y S E K J E N A K
U R F L L I A S I Y C V
Z I N L E A D E R X E A
B H L B F O C U S E I S
B O Y U F Z S T R O N G
G P M J D R E A M Y W B
W E W S M A R T X F A T
```

34

Fashion & Fun

Find these words:

RUNWAY, STYLE, OUTFIT, SPARKLE, ACCESSORY, POSE, GLAM, MIRROR, DRESS, HAIR

N M R A K L B L F W D I

Z G O C A R O U T F I T

G B J C N U D S I B S C

L T D E M N L Y F O P M

A Y M S J W G Y D P A I

M R S S E A W E U O R R

V L T O C Y K C G S K R

T Z Y R K O Y Q L E L O

R I L Y F H Z K F O E R

X C E B V B T F T D N H

N Y F C K Q C H A I R D

R Q D R E S S V A N V Z

Puzzle - Answers

Glamour Girl Vibes - Answer Key

```
G T C C O G K T R P G J
K G A O W L B Q T J E T
G W B N N U O U N X M P
R B A F N Q L E V V P B
O S V I D N D E A O O E
W H V D E X X N Z I W A
T I I E H X U W Y C E U
H N S N G J N Z W E R T
K E H C N V I V M K K I
O E E E F V Q Y X I S F
M I X E W L U A I N N U
N Z K E G O E Y M D F L
```

Friendship & Feelings - Answer Key

```
H A P O L O G I Z E H G
G P W I L I S T E N I U
Z U S N H O N E S T T B
G Z E C T L K N B L H O
Y B Q U R X H I Q R P N
L R X S U P P O R T G D
O S H R S N Q X G B E X
Y I J U T Z D E C L P J
A X J U E B G J B A T B
L R E S P E C T O U A K
E R H S C B A U U G L U
Q U R Z R G Q Q P H K G
```

Inner Power - Answer Key

```
T E Y W G A G U D V G C
E Y A O O B A V B M V I
M F Y R A R X I E M Z F
N Z F T L A U O Q F P Z
L O M H Y V W Y C I E Z
Q C V Y S E K J E N A K
U R F L L I A S I Y C V
Z I N L E A D E R X E A
B H L B F O C U S E I S
B O Y U F Z S T R O N G
G P M J D R E A M Y W B
W E W S M A R T X F A T
```

Fashion & Fun - Answer Key

```
N M R A K L B L F W D I
Z G O C A R O U T F I T
G B J C N U D S I B S C
L T D E M N L Y F O P M
A Y M S J W G Y D P A I
M R S S E A W E U O R R
V L T O C Y K C G S K R
T Z Y R K O Y Q L E L O
R I L Y F H Z K F O E R
X C E B V B T F T D N H
N Y F C K Q C H A I R D
R Q D R E S S V A N V Z
```

SHEvolves Power Words - Answer Key

```
E M P O W E R M E N T A
T L K I S A D G X H Z F
D W O R K S H O P U P G
X P U R P O S E L P R R
J O U R N A L V G P R O
D U B F Q V A O Q C R W
U B S J P P W L F Y P T
M E N T O R Y V S V X H
I N S P I R E E J A F W
G A F F I R M A T I O N
P V J J F D B S M W I F
D J S R O L E M O D E L
```

Testimonials

TESTIMONIAL BY 13 YEAR OLD TKYLA KELLY

Chanel showed me that jealousy and bad sportsmanship can hurt others but admitting your wrongs takes real courage. When she finally apologized, it taught me that growth starts with honesty. Glamour Girl is so real, I really enjoyed this" Chanel reminded me of a side of myself I don't always talk about. Sometimes it's hard to cheer for others when you want to win. What stood out to me was that even though no one called her out at first, when the truth was revealed, she owned up to her mistake and apologized. That part hit me because it showed me how strong it is to own your mistakes and grow from them. Glamour Girl isn't just about glam. It's real life.

41

TESTIMONIAL BY TAMARA JOHNSON
PRODUCTION ASSISTANT

"Glamour Girl" really hit home for me. It took me back to when I first started as a scuba diver, working in the photo and video department at my job. I was brand new, constantly seasick, and suddenly expected to learn two new dive skills while handling expensive gear all under pressure. It was tough, and honestly, there were moments I wasn't sure I'd make it. But I stuck with it. Two and a half years later, I had not only caught up with my coworkers, I was sometimes even ahead of them. I ended up setting project guidelines, became a confident diver, and was on the path to becoming a dive master. This story reminded me that growth is messy and challenging, but with determination and a little grace, you can really surprise yourself.

TESTIMONIAL BY 10 YEAR OLD KEYANNA WRIGHT STUDENT

I loved this story because it shows how Tia, who is my favorite character, didn't believe in herself at first. But once her friend told her she was good enough, she started to believe it too. I also liked how her confidence grew as she began the journey. It showed me that sometimes all it takes is someone believing in you to help you believe in yourself.

43

TESTIMONIAL BY KYZARIAH WILSON
COLLEGE SOPHOMORE

This story truly resonated with me. When I first began my journey in pageantry, I wasn't initially interested. It wasn't until a director saw something in me and presented me with an opportunity that everything changed. That moment led to my first success and from then on, I fell in love with the world of pageantry. Since then, I've gone on to claim six titles, three national and three international. Like Tia's story, my journey is a reminder that sometimes we don't realize our own potential until someone opens a door and we have the courage to walk through it.

TESTIMONIAL BY ANDREA KNOTT DIRECTOR OF BAHAMAS GALAXY PAGEANTS

It is more than a book, it is a movement; as a pageant director, I get to watch young girls trying to find their voice, confidence, and who they are. This story encapsulates that journey, through Tia's eyes, and it is inspiring, heartwarming, and relatable. All young girls, whether in pageantry or not, should read this novel; it will remind you that the real beauty begins from the inside.

TESTIMONIAL BY MRS GALAXY BAHAMAS 2024 RANDEIKA CARTWRIGHT

The book "Glamour Girl" was an amazing read. I enjoyed the emergence of Tia, a rather shy and reserved girl to stardom as she was recognized for her gift in modeling as she perfected her craft. The book teaches us that life is not free from self imposter syndrome and antagonists, but once we break free from the chains of oppression, we too can achieve all things we set out to do. With love.

TESTIMONIAL BY SHEVOLVES MEMBER & JR. TEEN BAHAMAS UNITED WORLD PAGEANTS TITLEHOLDER 2025 QUANELL HIGGS

Reading Glamour Girl was so real and relatable. It showed me that you don't need to have all the training or be perfect to stand out or succeed. What really stuck with me was the reminder not to sabotage yourself because even if others believe in you, it means nothing if you don't believe in yourself. This book helped me see that my confidence starts from within.

TESTIMONIAL BY EDUCATOR AND FOUNDER OF VALOR GIRL'S CLUB
VALENCIA HEPBURN

I like the storyline for a couple of reasons: The friend, "Kayla," is that person everyone should have in their corner. Sometimes, we can't see the good in ourselves, but having a sincere person who can see it, push us, and not be jealous of the gift is a blessing!
Also, the camaraderie of the girls "Mia, Tia, Lelia" shows there's usually more that' for you than against you. Find your tribe, be your own best self. This is an excellent read for girls who need that boost in self-esteem and the encouragement that they already have what it takes to do 'THE THING', whatever it is.